T0029421

FORTNITE BATTLE ROYALE HACKS

BUILDING STRATEGIES

FORTNITE BATTLE ROYALE HACKS

BUILDING STRATEGIES

AN UNOFFICIAL GUIDE TO TIPS AND TRICKS THAT OTHER GUIDES WON'T TEACH YOU

JASON R. RICH

Sky Pony Press
New York

This book is not authorized or sponsored by Epic Games, Inc. or any other person or entity owning or controlling rights in the Fortnite name, trademark, or copyrights.

Copyright © 2018 by Hollan Publishing, Inc.

Fortnite® is a registered trademark of Epic Games, Inc.

The Fortnite game is copyright © Epic Games, Inc.

All rights reserved. No part of this book may be reproduced in any manner without the express written consent of the publisher, except in the case of brief excerpts in critical reviews or articles. All inquiries should be addressed to Sky Pony Press, 307 West 36th Street, 11th Floor, New York, NY 10018.

Sky Pony Press books may be purchased in bulk at special discounts for sales promotion, corporate gifts, fund-raising, or educational purposes. Special editions can also be created to specifications. For details, contact the Special Sales Department, Sky Pony Press, 307 West 36th Street, 11th Floor, New York, NY 10018 or info@ skyhorsepublishing.com.

Sky Pony® is a registered trademark of Skyhorse Publishing, Inc.®, a Delaware corporation.

Visit our website at www.skyponypress.com.

Authors, books, and more at SkyPonyPressBlog.com.

10 9 8 7 6 5 4 3 2

Library of Congress Cataloging-in-Publication Data is available on file.

Cover design by Brian Peterson

Print ISBN: 978-1-5107-4338-0
Ebook ISBN: 978-1-5107-4339-7

Printed in the United States of America

TABLE OF CONTENTS

FORTNITE BATTLE ROYALE HACKS

BUILDING STRATEGIES

SECTION 1
YOUR QUEST FOR SURVIVAL IS ABOUT TO BEGIN!

What is it about *Fortnite: Battle Royale* that has allowed it to become the most popular game in the world, with more than 125 million active players? If you've already played this game on your PC, Mac, Xbox One, Playstation 4, Nintendo Switch, iPhone, iPad, or Android-based mobile device, you already know that it is an online-based multi-player game that takes place on a mysterious island. It's also fun and incredibly challenging to play!

While taking on the role of a soldier, your main objective, from the moment you land on the island, is survival! But to achieve this goal, you'll need to simultaneously handle multiple and equally important tasks throughout each intense match.

These tasks include:

- Avoiding the deadly storm that's spreading across the island.
- Safely exploring the island.
- Finding, collecting, and using a wide range of weapons and ammunition.
- Acquiring and using the best collection of loot items that can help you stay alive longer.
- Engaging in combat against up to 99 other enemy soldiers, without allowing any of them to defeat you.
- Collecting and gathering resources (wood, stone, and metal), which can be used to purchase items from the Vending Machines scattered throughout the island, but more importantly, to build.
- Building ramps, bridges, defensive structures, and often tall and sturdy fortresses throughout the match, and during the End Game.

Throughout this guide, screenshots from the Playstation 4 and Nintendo Switch versions of *Fortnite: Battle Royale* are showcased. Keep in mind, gameplay is virtually identical on all systems, although in some cases where information is displayed on the game screen varies slightly.

Do you have what it takes to survive on the island? You're about to find out!

The Importance of Building During a Match

In addition to providing a comprehensive overview of the entire *Fortnite: Battle Royale* game and offering hundreds of tips and expert strategies that'll help you survive during each match, so you successfully make it into the End Game, this guide teaches you how to become an expert builder. This means learning how to take full advantage of the game's Building mode.

Learning how to build within the *Fortnite: Battle Royale* game is only the first step. To become an expert builder requires practice . . . *a lot of practice.*

As you'll soon discover, there are three key steps to successful building. First, during an intense match, often while you're being attacked (as bullets and/or projectile weapons are traveling directly toward you), you must determine when and where to build.

Next, you'll need to figure out what to build, and which resources (wood, stone, and/or metal) to utilize. Finally, you'll need to skillfully switch between Combat mode and Building mode, and then actually do your building extremely quickly.

Particularly when you're being attacked, a fraction of a second will often mean the difference between successfully building a structure that'll protect you or being defeated by an opponent and getting eliminated from the match because you didn't build something to protect yourself fast enough.

As you're controlling your soldier during any match, you can either be in Combat mode or Building mode. This means you can either use your weapons to fight or be building at any given time. You can't do both tasks simultaneously.

Quickly switching between Combat mode and Building mode, and knowing when and how to make this switch, is an essential skill.

When in Combat mode, your soldier can switch between weapons within their personal arsenal, use one weapon at a time, use their pick-axe (to smash something or as a close-range weapon), use an item from their backpack, and move about (by walking, running, turning, crouching, tiptoeing, or jumping). Your soldier can also use emotes, access the island map, or view the backpack inventory screen. Other ways to get around include riding in an All Terrain Kart, walking into a Rift, or jumping into a Launch Pad or Bounce Pad.

While in Building mode, a soldier can move about, choose a building material, select what type of building tile to create (a wall, floor/ceiling, ramp/stairs, or roof piece), build the selected tile (using one resource at a time), edit something that's been built, access the island map, or access their backpack inventory screen. No weapon can be used, and the pickaxe can't be used as a weapon.

You'll Need to Build More Than Just Fortresses

Throughout a match, you'll encounter a wide range of challenges and obstacles that'll require you to do some building—long before you ever reach the End Game.

Anytime you're fighting against one or more opponents, the soldier who has a height advantage and the best weapons at their disposal often has the tactical advantage. Quickly building tall ramps to get up higher than an adversary is a common and often effective strategy.

One drawback to building a tall ramp to get a height advantage is that when an enemy shoots the bottom of your ramp with their weapon, especially an explosive weapon, the whole ramp will come crashing down with you still on it. Taking a fall less than three levels will result in injury, but a fall from higher up can be fatal. If you notice an enemy building their own ramp, instead of trying to shoot them while they're a moving target, focus on destroying their ramp while they're near the top of it.

Building a double ramp offers extra protection but uses more resources. This strategy allows you to jump between ramps as you're climbing upwards. Doing this makes it harder for an enemy to target your location, making you more difficult to hit. Plus, if the enemy tries to destroy one ramp, you can leap to the other to buy yourself a few extra seconds before you fall toward the ground.

Ramps can also be used to get to places you can't otherwise reach. For example, you can quickly climb up a steep cliff using a ramp. Keep in mind, you're able to enter into Building mode to build virtually anywhere on the island, including inside any other structure.

To reach the top of a cliff, instead of building a ramp that faces the cliff (like the one in the left screenshot above), the ramp will be stronger against attack if you build it sideways, along the side of the cliff. Ultimately, either ramp will make traveling to the top easier.

When you need cover overhead while building a ramp, construct an Over-Under Ramp. Instead of placing the building cursor along the ground where you want to build a regular ramp, place it in the center in front of you, and you'll create a ramp below your feet and above your head simultaneously.

Building an Over-Under Ramp requires extra resources, but it offers an additional protection from enemies positioned higher than you. Remember, having a height advantage during a firefight is usually beneficial.

If you're concerned that an enemy soldier might chase behind you as you run up a ramp, use one floor/ceiling tile on the ramp to create a platform, and on that platform, add a Trap. Then continue building your ramp and traveling along it. If the enemy soldier is not paying careful attention as they chase you, he or she will step on the Trap and go boom!

Walking through water is a slow process. You can speed it up and become less of a target if you keep jumping up and down while moving forward. However, the fastest way to cross over large bodies of water, like the lake found in Loot Lake, is to build a wooden bridge and run over it. If someone starts shooting at you, quickly build defensive walls to shield yourself.

There will be many times when you're wandering about the island and someone starts shooting at you. During these times, crouch down and hide behind a nearby object, and when possible, shoot back. Another option is to quickly build a defensive vertical wall, and immediately behind it, build a ramp. Then, crouch down behind this simple structure. An enemy will have to destroy two layers of protective shielding before reaching you.

To protect yourself from the sides as well, build walls on each side of the ramp tile, crouch down, and hide near the bottom of the ramp. How to build is covered within "Section 4—Becoming an Expert Builder."

Fortnite: Battle Royale Continues to Evolve

Epic Games frequently releases updates (called "patches") to *Fortnite: Battle Royale*. From each weekly or biweekly update, you can typically expect:

- New weapons and loot items to be introduced into the game.
- How certain weapons or loot items can be used are tweaked.
- Additions or changes are made to the points of interest (locations) on the island.
- New, but temporary, game play modes are introduced. These become available in addition to the Solo, Duos, and Squads game play modes.

For the first year of *Fortnite: Battle Royale*'s existence, building fortresses during the End Game (also known as the "Final Circle" portion of each match) was a particularly important skill to master. The players with the best collection of weapons, ammo, loot items, and resources, and who built the strongest and tallest fortress within the Final Circle always had the best tactical advantage.

While building continues to play an essential role when playing *Fortnite: Battle Royale*, the folks at Epic Games have begun to alter the game a bit—making it possible to focus on other strategies (beyond building), particularly during the End Game.

In addition to weekly or biweekly game updates, every three months or so, a new season of *Fortnite: Battle Royale* game play kicks off. In conjunction with each new season, Epic Games introduces some radical changes to the game. For example, entirely new points of interest are added, along with new weapons and loot items.

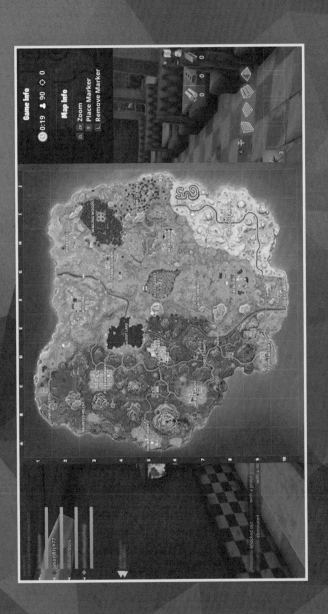

As you can see from the island map, there are approximately 20 labeled points of interest on the map, along with an ever-growing collection of other (unlabeled) locations that are well worth exploring. This is what the island map looked like at the start of Season 5 (July 2018). Each point of interest offers a different type of terrain, as well as different challenges to experience.

When Season 5 began, Epic Games altered the island rather dramatically. Anarchy Acres was replaced by Lazy Links, Moisty Mire was replaced by Paradise Palms, Dusty Divot (along with other points of interest) received a makeover, and many unlabeled points of interest were added, while others were redesigned or removed. Here's a view of Paradise Palms as a soldier freefalls from the Battle Bus. Notice what was formally Moisty Mire now has desert terrain.

Some points of interest are more popular than others. The popularity of a location helps to determine how many soldiers will initially land there after exiting the Battle Bus. If you want to land and be forced to participate in battles right away, choose a popular landing spot.

However, if you'd prefer to land in a more secluded spot and take time to gather resources and build up your arsenal before you're forced to fight, do not land within one of the labeled points of interest.

Also, anytime Epic Games introduces a new location to the island map, you can bet it'll be popular, since curious gamers will want to check it out, and more experienced players will want to see what's new on the island. As a noob (beginner), consider avoiding these new locations unless you're already well armed.

Instead, choose a landing spot that's more remote and less popular. Select a landing spot that you know offers nearby weapons, ammo, and loot items to quickly collect. This house on the coastline of the island, which has a large wooden tower on top of it. This house is in a remote location. And it's chock full of chests, weapons, ammo, and loot items. There are also plenty of nearby resources to harvest and collect. This house can be found between map coordinates I2.5 and J2.5.

Instead of landing directly in Tilted Towers, for example, land on this nearby hill and collect the weapons and loot items found in this hut.

Stopping at this hut before going into Tilted Towers allows you to enter into this very popular area with at least one weapon in your arsenal. You'll find similar structures just outside every popular point of interest. Slide down the cliff's edge (don't jump) to safely reach Tilted Towers from the hilltop hut.

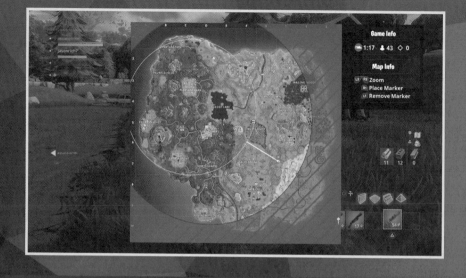

One potential drawback to landing in a remote location is that you may have a long way to travel to reach safety, once the storm starts expanding and moving. Your location is shown as a white triangle-shaped icon on the map. Here, the soldier is between map coordinates G7 and H7, but the circle that shows where the storm will be expanding to in about 77 seconds is off in the distance. This soldier needs to make a beeline toward Tilted Towers in order to remain safe. Using an All Terrain Kart or a Shopping Cart during the journey will certainly speed it up.

After looking at the island map before a match (while in the predeployment area or while aboard the Battle Bus), many of your fellow players will choose to exit the bus at the very start of the route the Battle Bus will take, or at the very end of the route. Others will head directly toward a popular point of interest. Again, to avoid encountering a bunch of enemy soldiers immediately upon landing, choose an alternate landing spot that's more remote.

Whenever something new is added to the game, look for a pop-up message like this one to appear when you launch the game. For more detailed information, visit: www.epicgames.com/fortnite/en-US/news.

What to Expect from Each Match

Each time you experience *Fortnite: Battle Royale* and choose the Solo game play mode, you'll have the opportunity to control a soldier who gets dropped off onto the mysterious island.

By selecting the Play option to enter into a match, you'll start off within the pre-deployment area as you wait for the Battle Bus to depart. You can roam around and interact with other soldiers freely. You can't be injured here. Anything you collect will be left behind once you board the Battle Bus.

Once aboard the Battle Bus, it will follow a random route over the island. Choose exactly when to leap from the bus to begin your freefall toward land.

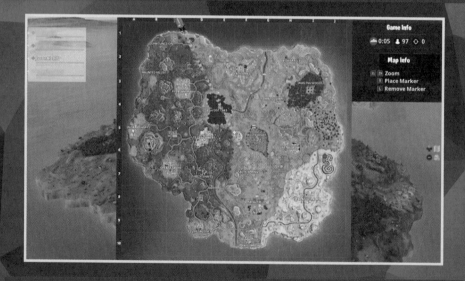

While in the pre-deployment area or when you first board the Battle Bus, access the island map to see the random route the bus will take over the island. The blue line (made up of arrows) shows you the route. Use this information to help you select the ideal landing spot on the island.

Initially when you depart the Battle Bus, you'll freefall toward land. Control the direction and speed of your descent and travel toward your desired landing location using your controller (or keyboard/mouse).

Using the directional controls, point your soldier downward during freefall to speed up his or her falling speed. It's always better to beat your competition to land, so you can be the first to grab a nearby weapon. If you're playing a Duos or Squads match, use Markers on the island map to pinpoint your intended landing spot. This creates a colored flare on the map (shown here), so your squad mates know where to land.

To ensure you don't land on the ground with a splat, shortly before you reach the island, your soldier's glider will automatically deploy. This slows down your rate of descent and gives you much more precise navigational control. Keep in mind, during freefall, you're able to activate (or deactivate) the glider until you get close to land (and it deploys by itself to ensure a safe landing). While players can choose an optional glider design, all gliders function exactly the same way.

Once you reach land, you'll be equipped only with a pickaxe. Your first objective is to find and grab a weapon, and to take cover so you don't get attacked while you're unarmed.

At the same time, up to 99 enemy soldiers land on the same island. To win a match, which lasts approximately 15 minutes, one soldier must become the sole survivor. Everyone else must be defeated and eliminated from the match. Ultimately, there's only one winner who achieves *#1 Victory Royale.* There's never a second or third place! This match was played in Squads mode. Three of the four squad members survived until the end.

Remember, as each soldier lands on the island at the start of a match, they're armed only with a pickaxe. This pickaxe can be used as a close-combat weapon to slash opponents, but its primary use is to harvest resources (wood, stone, and metal), and to help your soldier break apart objects.

Any wall, floor, or ceiling within a home, building, or structure can be smashed and destroyed, as can almost any object that's found on the island. When something is smashed by the pickaxe, depending on what it's made of, you'll collect either wood, stone, or metal. These are the resources you'll ultimately use for building. Here in Fatal Fields, for example, if you land on a silo and smash it, you'll generate metal and potentially find a chest.

Wood is the fastest to build with, but the weakest in terms of the level of attack it can withstand. Trees are an excellent source of wood. The larger and thicker the tree trunk, the more wood it will generate when smashed with a pickaxe. Stone allows you to build stronger ramps, walls, bridges, structures, and fortresses, but it's a bit slower to work with.

Metal is the strongest of the resources to build with, but it takes the longest to build with metal. There are several ways to harvest and collect metal, such as using the pickaxe to smash anything you encounter that's made from metal, including cars, trucks, buses, or RVs.

Each time you enter into Building mode, your first decision is to choose which resources to build with. Keep in mind, you can only build with resources you've already collected. If you have no resources, you can't build at all. As you'll discover from this guide, there are several ways to harvest and collect resources during each match.

Beware of the Deadly Storm

At the same time all of the soldiers are literally fighting for their survival, you'll need to contend with a deadly storm that forms on the island and slowly expands. While you can survive for short periods of time within the storm, eventually you'll perish if you spend too much time engulfed in the storm.

Shown here, a soldier is running through the storm, trying to reach a safe area of the island. Follow the white line that's displayed on the Location Map. This map is continuously displayed. Its location varies based on which gaming platform you're using. Here, it's in the top-right corner of the screen.

The longer your soldier remains within the storm, the greater the damage he or she will receive. Their Health meter will get depleted. Keep in mind, shields do not protect a soldier from the storm. Plus, during the later stages of a match, the damage inflicted when a soldier gets caught in the storm speeds up and increases.

Avoiding the storm altogether isn't always easy. As it continuously expands and takes over more and more of the island, it makes the land uninhabitable. If you get stuck within the storm and you have a Launch Pad on hand, use it to quickly travel a long distance and escape the storm. A Jet Pack, if currently available within the game, will also work to help you escape the storm, as will an All Terrain Kart or Shopping Cart.

Each time the storm expands and moves, all of the surviving soldiers are forced into a smaller and smaller circle (the eye of the storm), which contains the remaining safe area of land. When you view the island map, the areas displayed in pink have already been devastated by the storm. Within the outer circle is the current safe area of the island. The inner circle (when displayed) shows you where the storm will be moving and expanding to next, and where the safe area of the island will be. Use the timer displayed below the Location Map to determine when the storm will be moving next.

If you survive until the End Game (also known as the "Final Circle"), you'll discover that only a tiny circle of land on the island remains inhabitable and safe to occupy, and only a small number of enemy soldiers remain alive.

Because the remaining soldiers are forced into close proximity, everyone who is still standing is forced into combat, since only one person can remain alive for a match to end (when playing the Solo game play mode).

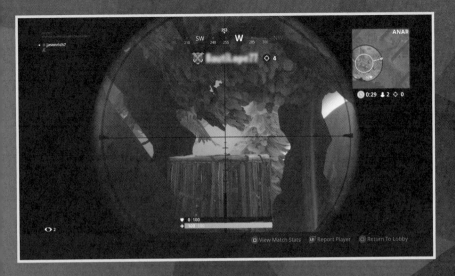

As you can see from the Location Map here (displayed in the top-right corner of the screen on a PS4), the circle has gotten very small, and will shrink again in 29 seconds. Only two soldiers remain in the match, and they're in close proximity to each other. One is on ground level and hiding behind a tree. The other soldier is better protected within a relatively small wooden fortress. The soldier who is hiding behind the tree is using a rifle with a scope to get a closer view of his adversary. As soon as this adversary pops his or her head up and becomes visible (even for a moment), the shooting will begin.

Surviving until the End Game will take skill, patience, and creativity. It'll also require you to continuously adapt your strategy and outsmart your opponents, since you'll need to defend yourself against up to 99 other soldiers, each of whom is being controlled by another gamer in real-time. As a result, every match you experience will be different.

How to Start Playing *Fortnite: Battle Royale*

One of the great things about *Fortnite: Battle Royale* is that anyone can play, on almost any gaming platform, yet everyone's experience is consistent.

To download and install the game on a PC or Mac, launch your favorite web browser and visit www.fortnite.com. Click on the yellow Download button that's displayed in the top-right corner of the browser window and follow the on-screen directions.

Xbox One players who have a paid Xbox Live Gold membership can sign into this online service and install *Fortnite: Battle Royale* onto their console for free. Playstation 4 players can download and install the game by accessing the online-based Playstation Store. A Playstation Network account is required to play. Nintendo Switch gamers can acquire the game from the online-based Nintendo eShop. A free My Nintendo account is required to play.

To experience *Fortnite: Battle Royale* on an Apple iPhone or iPad, download and install the *Fortnite* mobile app from the App Store using your Apple ID account. Meanwhile, Android-based mobile device users can obtain the game from the Google Play Store (starting in Summer 2018).

Depending on which system you're playing on, part of the game setup process typically requires setting up of a free Epic Games account. Visit https://accounts.epicgames.com/register to learn more.

For the most part, *Fortnite: Battle Royale* is cross-platform compatible. This means you can switch between playing on any gaming platform or competing against other players who are using different gaming platforms. As of July 2018, the exception to this was the Sony Playstation 4, which Sony refused to make cross-platform compatible with the Nintendo Switch.

Initially, acquiring the *Fortnite: Battle Royale* game is free, as is playing the game. As you'll discover from "Section 2—*Fortnite: Battle Royale* Offers In-Game Purchases," you can make several types of in-game purchases (which cost real money) in order to acquire and participate in Battle Passes and to customize the appearance of your character in the game.

What You Can Do from the Lobby

Once you launch the game, you'll find yourself in the Lobby. From here, you can handle a handful of game-related tasks, based on which command tab you select. They're displayed along the top-center of the screen. These main options include:

Lobby—From the Lobby, access any game-related option or menu, choose a game play mode, see some of your player stats, view a summary of Challenges, invite other players to participate (when experiencing certain game play modes), and enter into a match by selecting the Play option.

Battle Pass—Purchase an optional Battle Pass from this screen, view the Tier-based Challenges during the current *Fortnite: Battle Royale* season, or unlock the items offered by completing a Battle Pass Tier by making an in-game purchase (as opposed to completing the challenge). Purchasing a Battle Pass costs V-Bucks (in-game currency). Acquiring V-Bucks costs real money and can be done from the Store.

Challenges—View a complete listing of current Free Pass and Battle Pass Challenges.

Locker—From the Locker, customize your soldier's appearance using items you've purchased (one at a time from the Item Shop), as well as items you've unlocked by completing challenges. You can also acquire items, for free, from promotional partners, like Twitch.tv and Amazon Prime. For more information, visit: www.twitch.tv/prime/fortnite.

Item Shop—Each day, a different selection of rare or limited-edition outfits, pickaxe designs, back bling designs, glider designs, and emotes are available for sale from the Item Shop. As you'll discover in the next section, these optional items (which cost money) are used to customize the appearance of your soldier. These customizations are for appearance only, and do not impact your soldier's speed, agility, fighting capabilities, or what they can do within the game.

Store—Purchase bundles of V-Bucks that can be used to make in-game purchases. The more V-Bucks you purchase at once, the cheaper purchasing in-game items becomes, since a discount is offered. The price of 600 V-Bucks is $4.99 (US). Meanwhile, a bundle of 1,000 V-Bucks is priced at $9.99 (US). The cost of 2,800 V-Bucks is $24.99 (US), while 7,500 V-Bucks costs $59.99 (US). You can purchase 13,500 V-Bucks for $99.99 (US).

Customize Options from the Settings Menus

If you're new to playing *Fortnite: Battle Royale*, consider leaving most of the adjustable game options available from the Settings menus at their default settings. Later, as you get more acquainted with the game and develop your skills, you might choose to tweak some of these settings.

Often, expert *Fortnite: Battle Royale* gamers reveal their personalized game settings as part of their Twitch.tv live streams or YouTube videos. Don't just copy the settings of an expert gamer. If you're using a different gaming platform, it'll react differently. Meanwhile, if you're not as good of a player, adjusting the settings the wrong way could actually make you an even worse player. As you keep practicing to become a better player, tweak the various settings in ways that make the most sense for you personally, based on the strategies you typically use when playing.

To access the Settings menus, first access the game's Menu. The icon for it is displayed in the top-right corner of the Lobby screen. It looks like three horizontal lines. To access this menu, you'll need to press the Options button on the PS4 controller, or the "+" button on the Nintendo Switch controller, for example. Whenever there's an important announcement from Epic Games, it'll be displayed near the bottom-center of the Lobby screen.

Open the menu that's displayed near the top-right corner of the screen and select the gear-shaped Settings menu. A selection of submenus, starting with the Game Settings submenu is displayed. One at a time, scroll through the menus and make the feature adjustments you deem necessary.

From the Game Settings menu, new *Fortnite: Battle Royale* players should make sure features like Auto Equip Better Items, Aim Assist, Edit Mode Aim Assist, Turbo Building, Auto Material Change, and Controller Auto-Run are all turned on.

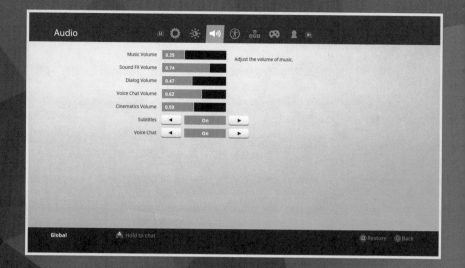

From the Sound submenu, you might opt to turn down the Music Volume, but turn up the Sound FX Volume, since the sound effects featured within the game are extremely important. For example, being able to hear an enemy soldier's footsteps will warn you when someone is approaching, often before you can actually see him.

To ensure you'll hear *Fortnite: Battle Royale*'s sound effects the way they were meant to be heard (and in a way that'll help you become a better player), seriously consider using an optional gaming headset (with a built-in microphone), or at least connect stereo headphones to your gaming system. A gaming headset will allow you to communicate with other players using your voice when experiencing one of the team-oriented game play modes, such as Duos or Squads.

Controller Layout Options

If you're using a controller on your Xbox One, PS4, or Nintendo Switch, for example, you're able to choose between several controller configurations from the Controller menu. Options include: Old School, Quick Builder, Combat Pro, or Builder Pro.

Choose whichever controller layout best fits your personal gaming style, and then memorize what each button does, so you can access the right command or function quickly during the game. Here are examples of the available controller layout options on a PS4 and Nintendo Switch. (When playing *Fortnite: Battle Royale* on a Nintendo Switch, using the optional Pro Controller is highly recommended for better control and shooting accuracy.)

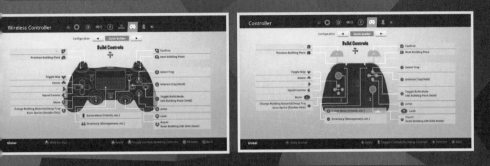

The Quick Builder controller layout on a Playstation 4 (Left).

The Quick Builder controller layout on a Nintendo Switch (Right).

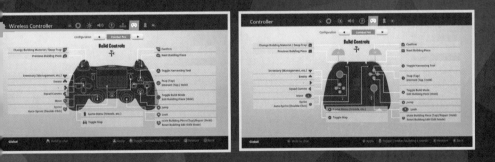

The Combat Pro controller layout on a Playstation 4 (Left).

The Combat Pro controller layout on a Nintendo Switch (Right).

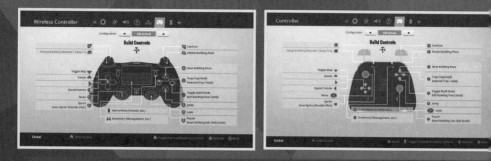

The Old School controller layout on a Playstation 4 (Left).

The Old School controller layout on a Nintendo Switch (Right).

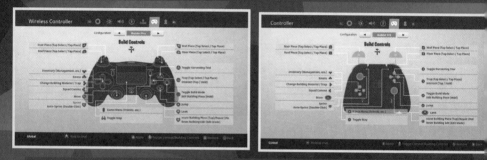

The Builder Pro controller layout on a Playstation 4 (Left).

The Builder Pro controller layout on a Nintendo Switch (Right).

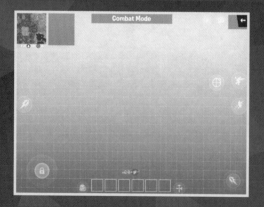

Similar controller layouts are available for the Xbox One. Mobile device users can choose between Combat Mode or Build Mode, and then customize the on-screen icons and buttons using this HUD Layout Tool, which is accessible when you access the Menu option from the Lobby.

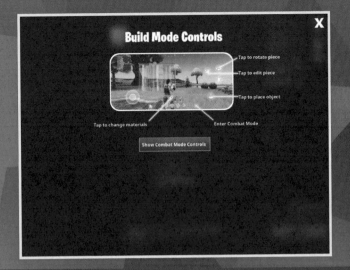

Here's the default layout for *Fortnite: Battle Royale*'s Build mode on a mobile device.

This is the default layout for Combat mode on a mobile device.

PC and Mac gamers can either use their mouse and keyboard to control the game, or take advantage of an optional game controller. When using the mouse and keyboard, you're able to assign specific game functions to specific keyboard keys or mouse buttons in order to further customize your game play experience.

SECTION 2

FORTNITE: BATTLE ROYALE OFFERS IN-GAME PURCHASES

Yes, *Fortnite: Battle Royale* is a free game to download, install, and play. But (yes, there's a but), optional in-game purchases are available, and these have proven to be extremely popular among gamers.

To make in-game purchases, start in the Lobby and scroll over to the Store tab that's displayed near the top of the screen.

From the Store, purchase V-Bucks using real money. The more V-Bucks you purchase at once, the larger discount you'll receive. Keep in mind, you can unlock a relatively small number of V-Bucks by completing Daily, Weekly, Free Pass, and Battle Pass-related challenges.

Once you've added V-Bucks to your game account, your current V-Bucks balance is displayed in the top-right corner of the Lobby, Battle Pass, Challenges, Locker, Item Shop, and Store screens. This in-game virtual money (which you used real money to acquire) is used to make in-game purchases. Remember, all available in-game purchases are optional. None are required to play *Fortnite: Battle Royale* on any gaming platform.

What You Need to Know About Battle Passes

In conjunction with the launch of each new *Fortnite: Battle Royale* season, Epic Games kicks off a new Battle Pass. These are divided into a series of tier-based challenges. Each time you complete a specific challenge or complete the group of challenges posed within a tier, you'll unlock items that can be used to customize your character. Other items, such as bonus XP, XP Multipliers, and 100 V-Buck bundles, are also sometimes offered as a prize for completing challenges.

During game play, you also have the ability to earn experience points (XP) by accomplishing certain tasks, like defeating an enemy, or completing specific in-game objectives (like dealing damage with a specific type of weapon or opening a specific number of chests within a particular point of interest). Earning experience points helps you boost your player level, and often helps you achieve certain Free Pass and Battle Pass-related challenges.

Everyone can participate in the Free Pass challenges for free (without purchasing a Battle Pass), but the items and prizes that can be unlocked by completing these challenges are not as rare or exciting as the ones offered to gamers who have completed Battle Pass-related challenges.

During each season, a Battle Pass can be purchased. It's best to purchase it right at the start of a new season, but it can be purchased anytime. Each costs 950 V-Bucks (at the start of a season, but then gets discounted a bit as a season progresses). Every three months or so, when a new gaming season begins, a new Battle Pass (offering new challenges) can be purchased, and the old one will expire.

To initially purchase a Battle Pass (after acquiring V-Bucks), from the Lobby, access the Battle Pass screen. In the lower-left corner of the screen, you'll see the Purchase option. Press the appropriate controller or keyboard button to make the purchase.

If you opt to purchase a Battle Pass, you have two choices. You can purchase just the Battle Pass or purchase the Battle Pass with 25 tiers unlocked (meaning that you automatically and immediately receive the prizes associated with those 25 tiers without having to complete the related challenges).

Upon confirming your purchase, the current Battle Pass will immediately be activated. (You'll be buying the Battle Pass for Season 5 or later.) If you've acquired the package that unlocks 25 tiers, one at a time, those prizes are awarded to you and unlocked within the game. Items that are unlocked will get stored in the Locker. XP bonuses, XP Multipliers, or V-Buck bundles will be added to your account.

A Battle Pass includes 100 tiers, each of which offers a prize once the challenges for that tier are completed. Prizes offered by the Season 5 Battle Pass, for example, include multiple outfits and emotes, along with many other awesome goodies.

Either from the left side of the Lobby screen, or by selecting the Challenges tab, you can view the current challenges, so you know what needs to be accomplished when playing *Fortnite: Battle Royale* moving forward.

How to Purchase Battle Pass Tiers

If a particular series of Battle Pass tier-related challenges is too difficult or time consuming, for 150 V-Bucks each, you're able to immediately unlock one tier at a time and receive those prizes. To do this, from the Lobby, return to the Battle Pass screen. In the lower-left corner, you'll see the Purchase Tier button. This only applies if you have already purchased the current Battle Pass.

Select the Purchase Tier option.

Confirm your purchase decision by pressing the appropriate controller button or keyboard key. The prize(s) associated with that tier will immediately be unlocked.

One of the great things about accomplishing daily, weekly, Free Pass, and Battle Pass tier-related challenges is that they don't just focus only on defeating enemies and winning matches. These challenges encourage you to accomplish other tasks within the game that often involve exploration, harvesting and collecting resources, finding and using specific loot items, or using a specific type of weapon.

Customizing Your Character's Appearance

One feature that gamers love in *Fortnite: Battle Royale* is the ability to customize the appearance of their soldier. This can be done by purchasing, unlocking, or acquiring individual items:

Choosing an Outfit

This is the clothing worn by your character. Every day within the Item Shop, several new outfits are released by Epic Games. The outfits offered as Featured Items tend to be rare or limited edition, and only available for a short time. Before each match, you're able to alter the appearance of your soldier if you've acquired optional items.

Individual outfits sold by the Item Shop cost between 500 and 2,000 V-bucks each. (This translates to between approximately $5.00 and $20.00 US.)

Here, the Dynamic Dribbler outfit is about to be purchased for 1,200 V-Bucks (approximately $12 US). All items you purchase, unlock, or acquire are yours to keep and use forever. They do not expire. You'll find your items within the Locker. From the Locker, you're able to choose which items you want to apply to your soldier. Only items you've purchased, unlocked, or acquired are available to you.

Check out this sample collection of previously released and popular outfits. Some are occasionally re-released in the Items Shop.

With its Asian theme, this Wukong outfit is considered "legendary" and ultra-rare.

The Cuddle Team Leader outfit is also "legendary" and rare, but it has a more whimsical appearance. Do you have the light-hearted and bubbly personality to rock it during a match?

At the same time Epic Games introduced the spray paint emotes into the game, this "Epic" Abstrakt outfit was also released.

Venturion is one of the slick-looking, more futuristic outfits that was made available for a limited time. It became an instant classic.

If you have a sweet tooth and enjoy candy, you'll love this Zoey outfit, which has a bright-colored candy theme.

The "legendary" Raven outfit is both sinister and mysterious looking. It's bound to strike some fear into enemies you encounter when your soldier wears it.

Who doesn't love pizza? Share your pizza passion by choosing the Tomatohead outfit. It's offered periodically for sale from the Item Shop. Add the optional pizza-delivery-box-themed back bling and the pizza cutter pickaxe design (sold separately), and you'll complete the look. Don't worry, you won't appear too cheesy wearing this optional outfit.

For gamers who want to add a touch of neon colors to their soldier's appearance, the Nitelite outfit is perfect. It was part of the Neon Glow set. When an outfit is part of a set, this means that a matching glider design, pickaxe design, and/or back bling design (each sold separately) was also released and made available for purchase.

Add Optional Back Bling to Your Character's Outfit

Typically, in conjunction with each outfit, a matching backpack design (back bling) is sold separately. Keep in mind, you can mix and match outfits with back bling, glider designs, and pickaxe designs from other sets to give your soldier an even more unique appearance.

Once you purchase, unlock, or acquire a back bling item, it becomes available from the Locker. When viewing the Locker screen, select the Back Bling slot to see the selection of back bling designs you own and that are available to you, and then choose one to apply to your character.

Choose a Glider Design

The glider is used when your soldier jumps from the Battle Bus at the start of a match and is activated to ensure a safe landing. During a match, a glider is also used when you take advantage of a launch pad item or walk into a Rift. While many different glider designs are available, all gliders function exactly the same way. None offers an advantage when used within the game.

Select a Pickaxe Design

At the start of a match, when your soldier lands on the island, he or she is armed only with their pickaxe. By purchasing, unlocking, or acquiring additional pickaxe designs, you can customize the appearance of this tool (and close combat weapon).

The pickaxe is seen and used often during a match. Regardless of which pickaxe design you select, they all function exactly the same way. In any house, for example, use the pickaxe to smash metal appliances in the kitchen to harvest metal.

Contrail Designs

Once your soldier leaps from the Battle Bus he or she begins their freefall toward land. If you've unlocked a contrail design, this is the animated graphic you'll see trailing behind them during their descent.

Contrail designs typically need to be unlocked by completing challenges. They're rarely, if ever, offered for sale from the Item Shop. They may, however, be offered as a free download as part of a free Twitch Prime Pack, for example, which is periodically offered to Amazon Prime subscribers who also have a free Twitch.tv account. Visit www.twitch.tv/prime/fortnite for more info.

Communicate Using Emotes

While you're visiting the pre-deployment area, or anytime during a match, one way to communicate with all other gamers in the same area as your soldier is to use an emote. *Fortnite: Battle Royale* offers several types of emotes, each of which must be purchased, unlocked, or acquired separately.

Dance Moves—Many different dance moves are available. They can be used separately, or you can create your own choreography by using several different dance moves back-to-back (in quick succession). Gamers often use dance moves as a greeting in the pre-deployment area, but during a match, they're often used to gloat about a victory or to taunt enemies.

Graphic Emotes—A large collection of individual graphic icons can be acquired and used. When one is selected, your soldier will toss it into the air for everyone around to see. The icon disappears after a few seconds.

Spray Paint Tags—Armed with a virtual spray paint can, your soldier can paint on any flat surface on the island, such as the ground or the side of a building. Many different spray paint tag designs are available separately.

Use one spray paint tag at a time or mix and match two or more of them to create interesting-looking graffiti on the island. Anytime you take time to use an emote, make sure it's safe to do so. You can't use a weapon at the same time you're using an emote, so you'll be vulnerable to attack during a match.

How to Acquire and Use Emotes

Each day, different dance moves, graphic emotes, and spray paint tag emotes are sold separately from the Item Shop. They typically cost between 500 and 800 V-Bucks each. They can also be unlocked by completing certain challenges or acquired as part of a Twitch Prime Pack.

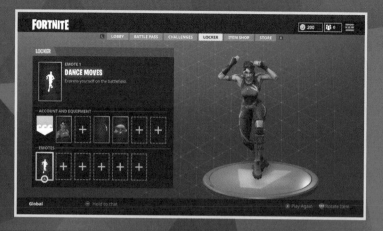

Before a match, equip your soldier with up to six different emotes. To do this, visit the Locker. Below the Emotes heading on the left side of the screen, you'll see six slots. Select and open one slot at a time.

Once you've selected an available slot, a listing of emotes that are available to you is displayed. This will include all of the dance moves, as well as the graphic emotes and spray paint tag designs available to you. When you select an emote that's displayed on the left side of the screen, a preview of it is showcased on the right side of the screen. Use the Save and Exit option to choose the selected emote for the slot that's active. Do this for each available emote slot, assuming you've acquired a collection of at least six different emotes. Here, a dance move is being selected.

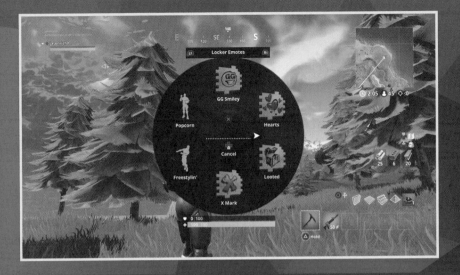

Whenever you're in the pre-deployment area before a match, or during any match, to use an emote, press the Emotes button on your controller or keyboard, and from the pop-up emotes menu that's displayed on the screen, choose the emote you want to use.

One way to use a dance move when you're playing a Duos or Squads match, for example, is to have one team member hide and prepare to launch a surprise attack on an enemy. Have another team member go out in the open and start dancing to attract attention. As soon as the enemy soldier reveals himself and tries to attack the dancer, his or her team member(s) can launch their attack on the enemies.

Once you defeat an enemy, assuming it's safe to do so, use a dance move to brag about your victory. The gamer you just defeated will likely see it from Spectator Mode, before he or she returns to the Lobby after being eliminated from the match.

SECTION 3

GET ACQUAINTED WITH THE ISLAND'S GEOGRAPHY

Every match you'll experience in *Fortnite: Battle Royale* takes place on the island. This is no ordinary island, however. It's chock full of interesting places to explore—each of which offers a unique setting where intense battles will unfold.

As Epic Games continues to release new weekly or biweekly updates, the game developer has continuously made alterations to the labeled and unlabeled points of interest on the map. When you begin playing *Fortnite: Battle Royale*, don't be surprised if there are new points of interest to explore, as well as dramatic changes made to preexisting points of interest you may already be familiar with.

The Island Map Displays Lots of Useful Information

Checking the island map during a match reveals a lot of useful information, including:

- The random route the Battle Bus will take across the island as it drops you off. This route is only displayed while you're in the pre-deployment area and for the first few seconds while aboard the Battle Bus.
- The location of each point of interest on the island.
- Your current location.
- The location of your teammate(s) if you're experiencing the Duos or Squads game play modes, for example.
- The current location of the storm.
- Where the storm will be expanding and moving to next.

If you're playing *Fortnite: Battle Royale* on a 4K resolution television set or high-definition computer monitor, whenever you look at the map in Season 5 or beyond, you'll see much more detail than ever before, especially when you zoom in on specific locations.

Each time you look at the full-screen island map, you'll discover it's divided into quadrants. Along the top of the map are the letters "A" through "J." Along the left edge of the map are the numbers "1" through "10." Each point of interest or location on the map can be found by its unique coordinates.

For example, Tilted Towers can be found at map coordinates D5.5, and Snobby Shores is located at coordinates A5. Lazy Links is located at F2.5, while the new racetrack can be found between coordinates I6.5 and J6.5. The main area of Paradise Palms is centered around coordinates I8.

When you check out the full-screen island map, you'll see at least 20 labeled points of interest, along with an ever-growing collection of other (unlabeled) areas that are definitely worth exploring. This is how the island map looked at the beginning of Season 5.

As you're looking at the island map, you're able to zoom in on specific areas to get a better look. In future versions of the game, Epic Games has said that the resolution of the map, especially when you zoom in, will improve greatly.

As each match progresses, check the large island map to see what areas of the island have already been engulfed by the storm. These areas are displayed in pink. The outer circle shows the current safe area.

When applicable, the inner circle on the island map shows where the safe area of the island will be once the storm expands and moves again. The timer that's displayed below the small map indicates when this will happen. You'll also see warnings about the storm displayed in the center of the screen. Plus, right before the storm is about to expand and move, you'll hear a ticking sound, followed by a unique storm warning sound effect.

Get Ready for Action Starting When You Land

When you land within a popular point of interest, like Tilted Towers, you'll almost definitely encounter enemy soldiers within seconds. Upon landing, take cover and quickly find and grab a weapon, so you'll be able to fight. Otherwise, you'll often be shot and defeated almost immediately upon landing.

You can count on having to engage in fights when visiting the more popular points of interest. Instead of landing directly in one of these places, consider landing in the outskirts. This is a view from outside of Tilted Towers. Collect weapons, ammo, and/or loot items from surrounding structures and areas, and then enter into the point of interest on foot when you're better armed and prepared to fight. In Tilted Towers, for example, as soon as you grab a weapon, don't stay out in the open. Smash the roof with your pickaxe, so you can drop into a building you landed on. Going indoors offers more cover and protection from enemy fire (unless there's an enemy in the building with you).

If you land in a popular area and immediately encounter other soldiers, consider rushing them with your pickaxe and launching an attack. You'll need to make several direct hits with the pickaxe to defeat an enemy. Keep jumping around and moving in between pickaxe swings to avoid getting hit by the opponent's pickaxe attacks. However, if the adversary landed a few seconds before you and managed to grab a nearby weapon, run away before you get shot. Here, the soldier holding the pickaxe was too slow for the enemy armed with a weapon.

Be on the Constant Lookout for Chests, Supply Drops, and Loot Llamas

Throughout the island—mainly within buildings, homes, and other structures, as well as inside of trucks, but sometimes out in the open—you'll discover chests. They have a golden glow and make a sound when you get close to them. Open chests to collect a random selection of weapons, ammo, loot items, and resources. To collect a chest's contents, you must be the first soldier to open it during a match.

Some chests are usually found within the same spot on the map, although this too is changing as Epic Games releases new game updates. Sometimes, chests randomly appear during each match, so always be on the lookout for them (and listen carefully for the sound they make).

As you're exploring various areas, listen closely for the unique sound chests emit. You'll often hear this sound before a chest comes into view. Assuming it's safe, approach the chest and open it. Then be ready to grab the items you want or need.

At random times during a match, you may be lucky enough to spot a Supply Drop. This is a floating balloon with a wooden crate attached. They're somewhat rare. If you spot one, approach with caution, and open the crate. Inside you'll discover a random selection of weapons, loot items, ammo, and resource icons.

To protect yourself as you approach a Supply Drop (as well as a chest or Loot Llama), quickly build walls around yourself and the object.

An even rarer object to come across on the island is a Loot Llama. This colorful item looks like a piñata. Smash it open and you'll discover a collection of random weapons, ammo, loot items, and resource icons. Typically, the weapons found within Loot Llamas are rare and often "legendary."

Another strategy instead of opening a Loot Llama, for example, is to place remote explosives on it and then hide. As soon as an enemy soldier approaches, manually detonate the explosives to defeat the enemy. As you approach a Supply Drop or Loot Llama, consider quickly building walls around yourself and the object, so you're protected before opening the crate or smashing the Loot Llama.

Another way to quickly build up your arsenal is to buy rare and powerful weapons from Vending Machines. These can be found in random locations on the island. If you've gathered enough resources (wood, stone, or metal), exchange them for useful weapons or loot items.

If you don't yet have enough resources to purchase the item(s) you want, go out and collect more wood, stone, or metal, and then return to the Vending Machine. Keep in mind, when you're standing in front of a Vending Machine, you're vulnerable to attack. Consider building walls to surround your soldier and the machine. Otherwise, as soon as you make a purchase, a nearby enemy might launch a surprise attack, defeat you, and quickly collect everything you've purchased and gathered during the match.

Prepare Yourself for Whatever Terrain You Encounter

Whether you're exploring one of the labeled points of interest on the map, or you're traveling in between points of interest in order to avoid the storm or to explore, you are going to encounter many different types of terrain.

Several areas on the island are comprised of farmland. In these locations, you'll discover a primarily flat landscape with barns, farmhouses, silos, horse stables, and other structures to explore. There's often a lot of open space between these structures (which includes planted crops that have since wilted or perished). Travel quickly in between the structures, so you're not an easy target to shoot at, and be sure to explore all levels of the various buildings and structures you encounter.

Anytime you enter into a building, house, or structure, be ready to explore inside. You'll likely find chests, as well as weapons, ammo, loot items, and/or resource icons lying out in the open. Within houses, chests are most often found in the attic, basement, or garage. Weapons, ammo, loot items, and resource icons are more typically found lying on the ground, out in the open, within various rooms. Most houses on the island look unique; however, you can explore each of them the same way.

Whenever you notice an outside cellar door as you approach a house, smash it open and explore the basement. You're almost guaranteed to find a chest, along with other weapons, ammo, loot items, and perhaps resource icons lying out in the open.

Ammo can also be found within green ammo boxes. These don't glow like a chest, nor do they make a sound. But when you open one, you're provided with a selection of ammo you can grab. Sometimes ammo boxes will be hidden under staircases, on shelves, or behind furniture or other objects.

Inside homes, buildings, or structures, don't be surprised if you encounter enemy soldiers. As you enter a building, listen carefully for footsteps, as well as for the opening and closing of doors, or for items being smashed. If you hear someone else inside, you have several options. For example, you can:

- Leave the area and find someplace else to explore.

- Enter with your weapon drawn and be prepared to engage in battle.
- Peek through a window and shoot at an enemy from outside, or toss a grenade, clinger, or another explosive weapon through the window.
- Wait outside, preferably hidden, and then attack the enemy as he or she leaves.

Instead of entering a building, house, or structure using the front door, consider entering through a back door or the garage, if applicable, so maybe you can surprise whoever is inside. Keep in mind, the inside of structures offers many potential hiding places.

After you enter into a structure or an individual room, close the door behind you. Then if you anticipate an enemy soldier following you, hide behind an object, crouch down, and aim your weapon toward the door. As soon as the enemy enters, start shooting.

Another option is to booby trap a room within a house, building, or structure using remote explosives or traps, for example. Then, when an enemy enters, they'll receive a surprise blast. Just make sure you're far enough away from the explosion so you don't get injured by your own explosive weapon attack.

From outside of a building or structure, throw grenades through a window, an open door, or hole in a wall or ceiling to blow up whoever is lurking inside. Just make sure your soldier doesn't get caught in the blast as well.

Don't forget, you're able to build ramps, walls, or use other building tiles inside of preexisting structures, or you can build onto an existing structure. For example, you can build a ramp to help you reach an attic that's otherwise not accessible from inside (shown here), or you can build a mini-fortress around yourself in the middle of a room.

It's also possible to build a ramp or fortress on top of a preexisting structure. This one was built on top of the structure located in the center of Pleasant Park.

Standing at the top of the fortress that was built on the roof of the structure in the center of Pleasant Park offers a great 360-degree view of the surrounding area.

Just about anything you encounter on the island can be smashed with the pickaxe, shot at (and destroyed if you hit it with enough ammo), or demolished using explosives. This includes buildings, homes (or parts of homes, like a garage door), and other structures. If you notice an enemy hiding within a building, instead of going inside to fight, use a projectile explosive, such as a grenade launcher or rocket launcher, and blow up the entire structure with your enemy still inside.

By using the pickaxe to smash objects, such as the house's garage door, you simultaneously harvest resources (wood, stone, or metal). However, if you blow something up with an explosive weapon or shoot at it in order to destroy it, you won't collect any resources.

Whenever you open a door within a structure that may already be inhabited, have your weapon drawn and be ready to fire. Scan the room quickly, grab what you want if there's something worthwhile inside, and then move on to the next room.

Anytime you need to travel across open terrain (as you move between buildings at the racetrack, for example), you're typically vulnerable to attack. To reach your destination safely, run in a random, zig-zag pattern (don't walk), and keep jumping to make yourself a fast-moving target that's harder to hit. If you do start getting shot at, quickly hide behind a nearby object or build protective walls around yourself to serve as shielding.

Instead of traveling at ground level across wide open terrain, consider building a ramp to get yourself higher up, and then build a bridge that takes you in the direction you need to go.

For example, build a ramp between the roofs of two or more buildings. This will require a bunch of resources, but it'll potentially keep you higher than your adversaries, which gives you a tactical advantage in a firefight.

When exploring a multi-story building, be sure to enter into the small rooms to discover what might be available to grab within them. Some buildings, houses, and churches, for example, have hidden rooms. You'll sometimes need to use the pickaxe to smash through walls, floors, or ceilings to discover these rooms, and then see what's inside.

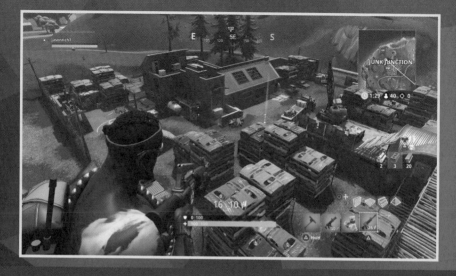

When visiting areas like Junk Junction (found at map coordinates B1.5), expect to encounter large piles of demolished cars that create a maze-like area to navigate through at ground level. There are also storage facilities on the island that contain many large cargo containers that create mazelike areas. Try to avoid staying on ground level. Climb on top of the car piles or cargo containers, so you can shoot at enemies below you and see all around.

The ground level of mazelike areas is a great place to plan and execute sneak attacks or to ambush enemies. You can also set traps or use remote explosives to blow up enemies who pass by.

Within Lonely Lodge and in other areas of the island, you'll encounter cabins and other small, stand-alone structures. Hide inside any of them and close the door behind you. As soon as an enemy opens the door, be ready to blast them with one of your most powerful guns. Another strategy is to place a trap inside one of these smaller structures, set it, and then close the door (if applicable) as you leave. The next person will be greeted with a bang!

Remember, anytime you approach a house, building, or structure, and you notice the front door is already open, someone else has been there before you, and they could be hiding inside and waiting to attack you. Plus, any chests, ammo boxes, or other loot items that were in the structure have likely already been rummaged through.

If you opt to directly cross a large body of water, like Loot Lake, don't just walk through it. This will be very slow and leave you out in the open and vulnerable to attack. Instead, build a wooden bridge to cross it, and then move quickly. Be ready to build walls around yourself as shielding if you get shot at by someone sniping you from land. Instead of crossing the lake yourself, if you have a sniper rifle (or any weapon with a scope), find a secure hiding spot along the edge of the lake (or swamp), and then pick off other soldiers that attempt to cross when they're out in the open and fully exposed.

Don't get too distracted by exploration. Always pay attention to the location of the storm and the direction it'll be moving next. Here, the soldier has a long way to travel to get out of the storm. His Health meter is almost depleted, and he has no HP powerups or a Launch Pad, for example, to replenish his health or speed up his journey. Because this gamer wasn't paying attention to the storm, his soldier is about to perish, despite having collected a great arsenal of weapons and ammo.

Since you're able to survive in the storm for short periods of time, assuming your Health meter isn't close to being depleted, you can enter into the storm on purpose, and then reemerge outside of the storm, behind an opponent, to launch a surprise attack. Hide within the storm to reposition yourself, if necessary. A good gamer will know to watch their back when it's to the storm, but a noob won't expect someone to exit from the storm with the sole purpose of attacking.

You never know when or where you'll come across a chest. The large building with a pink tree growing in the center of Lucky Landing, for example, often (but not always) has a chest hidden within the tree trunk. Smash the giant tree to reveal it.

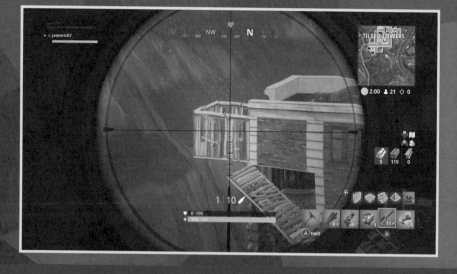

Just about anywhere you are on the island, to get a bird's-eye view of what's around you, and to get higher up than enemies, consider building a ramp. Fortify the bottom of the ramp, so if an enemy tries to destroy it, you won't instantly come crashing down. Use a weapon with a scope to zoom in and see what your enemies are up to, and when they become visible, shoot 'em.

Anytime you're in an area that contains shops or restaurants, always check behind the counters. You never know what's waiting to be collected.

Bridges that lead in and out of points of interest, like Lucky Landing, are also places where you're apt to stumble upon chests, as well as weapons, ammo, loot items, and/or resource icons that are lying out in the open. Search below the bridges as well.

There are several suburban communities found throughout the island that contain groups of single-family houses (along with other smaller structures). Search each home as you see fit and to build up your arsenal, but beware of enemy soldiers hiding out inside. Instead of traveling along at ground level to move between houses that are close together, go to a higher level (or the roof) and build a bridge between two houses or structures, so you can stay up high. To reach a house's attic easily, land on its roof, build a ramp from the outside or from the inside, start at ground level and work your way upward. It is often easier to reach the outside of a house's roof and then smash your way into the attic from above.

Many of the suburban areas include an outdoor soccer field or park. In other words, a large, open space. Sometimes, you'll discover something worth grabbing in the center of one of these open spaces. If you choose to approach it, do so with extreme caution. Enemy snipers will likely try to shoot at you, and you'll be out in the open and vulnerable to attack.

Anytime you discover a water tower (like the one found at the edge of Retail Row) or a silo (like these two in Fatal Fields), smash it. You'll typically find a chest or other useful weapons. You'll also stock up on some metal by smashing the tower or silo.

Wherever your exploration takes you on the island, when you encounter broken down cars, trucks, buses, RVs, tractors, or other types of vehicles, you have the option to smash them and harvest metal.

Hiding behind any type of vehicle when you're being shot at or trying to avoid enemy contact is another way to take advantage of the many broken down vehicles found on the island.

Remember, when you smash cars, it makes a lot of noise. To make matters worse, the car's alarm will often activate and generate even more noise. This will definitely attract attention and alert nearby enemies to your location.

Be sure to check within and above the larger trucks and vehicles for chests or other weapons, and then decide if you want to harvest some metal by smashing these larger vehicles.

There are places on the island that contain underground tunnels (or mine shafts), like Shifty Shafts. The mine tunnels follow a mazelike design, so you can't see around turns. Listen carefully for footsteps. Don't get surprised and attacked by enemies. It's best to crouch down and tiptoe through this area, so you make the least amount of noise possible.

In popular and heavily congested places like Tilted Towers, it's dangerous to be outside and at ground level, because enemies can shoot at you from the higher levels of buildings that surround you. If you find yourself on ground level in a densely populated area, be ready to crouch behind vehicles or objects for protection if someone starts shooting at you.

Instead of staying at ground level, you're typically better off staying inside a building, as high up as possible. Using your mid- to long-range weapons (preferably with a scope) look out a window and shoot at enemies below from a safe distance. Don't forget, you can shoot or be shot at through windows. Enemy soldiers can also enter the building you're in at any time, so if your back will be to a door inside, consider building a wall for extra shielding in case someone tries to enter.

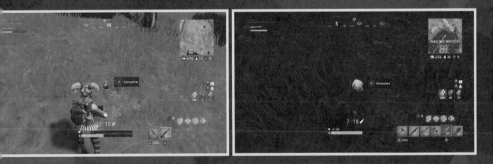

When traveling through the dense forest areas of the island, smash down trees to collect wood. Also keep an eye out for apples on the ground. If you spot an apple, grab it and eat it. This will replenish five points (up to 100) on your soldier's Health meter. When in swampy areas, look for blue mushrooms on the ground. These will replenish five points (up to 100) on your soldier's Shield meter.

As you explore the island, you'll encounter many steep cliffs. Never jump off a cliff, or you could injure yourself or even perish. Instead, slide down the edge of a cliff, and you'll land safely on the ground.

If you need to travel a great distance quickly, to avoid an attack or out-run the storm, for example, consider using a Landing Pad, All Terrain Kart, or a Shopping Cart. When you step onto a Landing Pad, you get catapulted into the air, and can travel a far distance. Your glider will activate and allow you to steer your soldier safely back to land.

Shopping Carts are rare, but if you find one, you can push it up a hill, hop into it, and then ride it down a hill and cover a lot of territory quickly. Shopping Carts have been added and removed from the game multiple times, and what can be done with them continues to change periodically.

Anytime you stumble across a pile of tires, you can't smash or collect them, but you can jump on them. When you jump on tires, you're catapulted up extra high into the air.

Discover Some of the Island's Unlabeled Areas

As you travel between labeled points of interest, or if you choose to roam freely around the island, you're sure to encounter many interesting places. Here are a few spots you don't want to miss. With each new game revision, you'll likely discover at least a few new places to explore that aren't labeled on the map. Some of the places described in this section may be removed (or replaced with others) as time goes on.

There's a small Western town located at the edge of the island, between Paradise Palms and Lucky Landing (near map coordinates H9). This area offers a bunch of buildings to explore, many of which have chests to open, or at least weapons, ammo, and loot items to collect.

If you're lucky, you'll discover an All Terrain Kart near the entrance/exit of this town. When you're done exploring here, hop in the golf cart and follow the paved road to Paradise Palms, or go off-roading to any other destination on the island.

Between map coordinates D2 and E2, you'll discover an abandoned motel. The guest rooms and the structures surrounding the main motel area are worth visiting if you want to expand your arsenal and stock up on ammo.

Found at map coordinates I5.5, you'll discover this RV park. Hidden between the RVs you'll find some useful things to pick up, but the really good stuff can be found in the buildings that surround this fenced-in area. Stand on top of the RVs and jump from one to the other in order to maintain a height advantage in case enemy soldiers are lurking about. Smash the RVs to collect a lot of metal.

Here at map coordinates D8, you'll come across a giant wooden chair, along with a few buildings and homes that are worth taking a few minutes to explore.

At map coordinates E9, you'll encounter a cluster of buildings, including an abandoned dance club. Take a moment to practice your dance moves on the dance floor but be careful you don't get sniped or flanked by an enemy. Chests are located in other areas of this building (including sometimes behind the DJ booth), so search carefully and be thorough. Don't neglect exploring the neighboring buildings and structures as well, while you're in the area.

Be sure to visit map coordinates H4.5 to discover this cargo storage facility. Here there's a mazelike area of storage containers, as well as several buildings to explore. There are multiple chests to be found in this region. Try to stay higher up, so you can snipe at enemy soldiers you may encounter below you. Once you have a weapon, try walking along the overhead scaffolding that goes across this area. As always, another option is to build a ramp that takes you higher than your adversaries.

There Are Strange-Shaped Watch Towers Around the Outskirts of the Island

Along the coastline of the island, you'll discover a small collection of massive wooden watch towers that are shaped like different animals and objects. Consider landing on top of any of these towers and smashing your way down to discover chests and other useful weapons, ammo, and loot items. If you're approaching any of them on foot, you can always smash your way inside and climb upward using pre-created stairs or ramps you build yourself.

There's a llama-shaped tower at map coordinates B1.5, just outside of Junk Junction.

While it's a bit out of the way, there's a large wooden tower located between I5 and J5.

As you climb the tower, grab the weapons and ammo you discover lying out in the open, on the stairwell.

When you reach the top, go into the hut and you'll discover a chest.

From the top of the wooden tower, you'll catch an amazing view of Paradise Palms and its surrounding desert area. Keep an eye on where the storm is traveling, so you don't get caught in its path.

Located between map coordinates I2.5 and J2.5 is this house with a large wooden tower above it. There are chests and plenty of other useful weapons, ammo, and loot items to be found here. It's a nice, remote place to land and quickly build up your arsenal.

How to Choose the Ideal Landing Location

One of the very first decisions you'll need to make at the start of each match is where on the island you want to land. First, while you're hanging out in the pre-deployment area, or when you first board the Battle Bus, check out the island map that shows the random route across the island that the bus will take.

When choosing a landing location, here are some things to consider:

- Do you want to land within one of the popular points of interest, knowing that you'll likely encounter enemy soldiers and need to fight almost immediately? If you choose this option, you'll need to find a weapon and be prepared to fight within seconds after landing.
- If you plan to land within one of the newly added points of interest, whether or not it's labeled on the island map, it's going to be a popular landing destination. Gamers always want to check out what's new. Thus, you'll definitely encounter enemy soldiers immediately upon landing.
- Out of the up to 99 other gamers participating in each match, many will jump from the Battle Bus at the very start of its journey across the island. Others will wait until the very last second before taking their leap off the bus. As a result, whatever points of interest are close to the start or end of the bus route will be popular during that match.
- Points of interest near the center of the island always tend to be popular. Many of the routes the Battle Bus could take go directly over this area, plus when you start a match near the center of the island, you typically don't have to travel as much to stay clear of the storm once it begins to expand.

As you're making your final approach toward land and looking for a building or structure to land on, look for the golden glow of a chest. Sometimes, you can see this glow emanating from a hole in a building or house's roof.

A common strategy amongst expert *Fortnite: Battle Royale* players is to land in an unpopular spot where they'll likely find an abundance of weapons, ammo, and loot items right away. For example, the roof of the house located at the edge of the island, between map coordinates I2.5 and J2.5.

After quickly building up your arsenal, travel inward, avoiding the storm and any popular points of interest until you're close to the Final Circle and the End Game. Along the way, collect an abundance of resources (wood, stone, and metal), and be sure to search the buildings and structures you encounter.

By avoiding any points of interest early on, you dramatically decrease your chances of encountering enemy soldiers and being forced to fight. Instead, you can focus on building up the perfect arsenal for the End Game, while stocking up on supplies and resources. You won't earn as many experience points taking this approach, but you'll likely stay alive longer during each match.

SECTION 4

BECOMING AN EXPERT BUILDER

As you know, building can play a crucial role in your success when playing *Fortnite: Battle Royale*. The truth is, you can often get away with doing very little building during a match, and still do extremely well. However, by perfecting your building skills, and just as importantly, your building speed, you'll definitely have an advantage and become a better all-around *Fortnite: Battle Royale* player.

You can read about how to build, and you can watch videos on YouTube, as well as live streams on Twitch.tv to get ideas about how and what other *Fortnite: Battle Royale* players build, but nothing replaces the need to practice building. You'll never become a fast builder unless you practice. To become an expert builder will require a lot of practice.

Many expert *Fortnite: Battle Royale* players agree that building is somewhat faster and easier when playing the PC or Mac version of the game, using a keyboard and mouse. But, if you practice enough using a game controller, or the touchscreen on your mobile device, you can still perfect your building skills and building speed to become a worthy adversary to even the best players. (Most of the screenshots featured in this section were taken on a Nintendo Switch.)

Ways to Gather the Resources You'll Need

The more resources you harvest or collect during a match, the more building you'll be able to do. Without resources, however, you're unable to build anything. At the start of a match, you'll have zero resources.

When playing most versions of *Fortnite: Battle Royale*, the amount of wood, stone, and metal you currently have is displayed along the right side of the screen. Look for the Wood, Stone, and Metal icons with numbers below them. (The location may vary, based on the gaming platform you're using.)

During a match, there are four primary ways to harvest and collect wood, stone, and metal, including:

- Use your soldier's pickaxe to smash objects and harvest resources.
- Collect resource icons. They can be found out in the open (often lying on the ground).
- Defeat an enemy and collect the resources he or she was carrying. Especially during the later stages of a match, this is a quick way to really increase your resources.
- Collect resource icons from chests, supply drops, and Loot Llamas. Each of these will significantly boost your resources.

Anything made of wood that you smash will generate wood resources. Trees, wooden pallets, and the walls, floors, or roofs of many houses, buildings, and structures are all great sources of wood. The larger the tree and the thicker its trunk, the more wood you'll harvest by smashing it. The largest trees tend to be found within Wailing Woods. Wood is the most abundant and easily accessible resource on the island.

Smashing rock formations with the pickaxe is one way to generate stone. You can also smash brick buildings, or other stone objects (such as the churches or tombstones found in Haunted Hills).

Smashing metal objects, including appliances in homes, machinery in buildings, any type of vehicle, or large metal storage containers are all great sources of metal.

This is what a Wood icon looks like. Grab it and your wood resource goes up by 20.

When you come across a Stone icon, which looks like a brick, grab it. You'll receive a small bundle of that resource. The small yellow icon displayed on the item name banner says how much of the resource you'll collect. In this case, it's x20 stone, which is typical for resource icons found lying out in the open, on the ground, for example.

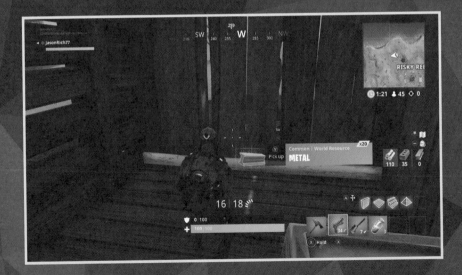

Find and grab Metal icons to increase your stash of metal.

Basic Building Strategies

In order to build, you'll need to put away your weapons (and pickaxe) and enter into Building mode. Switching between Combat and Building mode is done by pressing the appropriate game controller button (or the appropriate keyboard or mouse button if you're playing on a computer).

Once in Building mode, there are two choices you'll need to make immediately. First, which resource you want to build with. Second, which shape building tile you want to create. By mixing and matching the four building shapes, you can build walls, ramps/stairs, bridges, basic fortress, or extremely elaborate fortresses, depending on your need, creativity, and available resources.

The four building tile shapes include:

Vertical wall tiles. After selecting a building resource and a tile shape, a translucent version of the building tiles is displayed. Use the directional controls to choose the desired location before pressing the Build button.

As soon as you press the Build button, the selected and placed tile is built using the chosen material. At this point, while still in Building mode, have your soldier face the tile and enter into Edit mode to alter the tile. For example, you can add a door or window.

While the building tile is still translucent, the information displayed near the center of the tile before it's actually built tells you how much of the selected resource is needed to build that tile. In this case, it's 10 wood. You'll also discover that once built, the vertical wall tile will have 200 HP. While the selected building tile is still translucent, you can still reposition it, rotate it, or change the building material using your controller or keyboard commands.

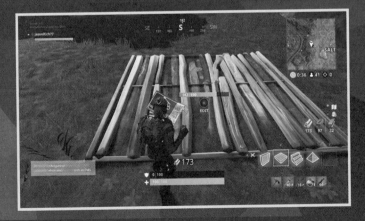

Here, a single floor/ceiling tile is actually in the process of being built out of wood.

This is a wooden ramp tile being positioned before it's actually built. When building with wood, and the ramp/stairs-shaped tile is selected, ramps are automatically created.

Shown here is a single ramp tile. It goes up one level. The more ramp tiles you connect, the higher up the ramp will go. As you're walking (or running) up the ramp, keep building to get higher.

When building with stone or metal, after selecting the ramp/stairs tile shape, stairs are automatically constructed, but at a slower rate. Anything built with stone is stronger than wood, and anything built with metal is even stronger. This stone staircase, for example, offers 280 HP. Each stone tile in this staircase required 10 stone to construct.

This staircase built from metal has 370 HP. Each metal stair-shaped tile required 10 metal to construct. Keep in mind, how much HP each tile has periodically changes as Epic Games tweaks the building aspects of the game.

As soon as you start building any tile, an HP meter is displayed, and that tile begins offering protective shielding against an attack. The HP meter starts out displayed in orange to show that the tile is not completed. It then turns green when it's been fully constructed. Remember, until the tile is fully constructed, it does not have its full HP, so it does not offer its maximum protection. Here, the partially built stone staircase currently offers 147 HP out of 280 HP.

Pyramid-shaped tiles can be used to hide behind, or as a roof for your structures and fortresses. This type of tile made from wood offers 190 HP and costs 10 wood each to construct. If the same tile were made from stone, once completed, it could withstand 280 HP worth of damage. One pyramid-shaped tile made with metal (which costs 10 metal to build), however, can withstand 370 HP worth of damage.

This wooden structure was built using one floor tile and four vertical wall tiles. One pyramid-shaped tile was used for the roof. Once the core structure was built, a door was then added, making it easy for the soldier to enter and exit.

One of the most basic structures you're able to build, and the one you're likely to use most frequently is a multi-tile ramp that goes up two or more levels. This ramp was constructed using multiple wood ramp/ stair tiles. The more tiles you use, the taller your ramp (or staircase) becomes, but the more resources you'll need to build it.

Remember, the main drawback to building and using a tall ramp is that an enemy can shoot at and destroy the bottom tile (or any tile in the middle), and the whole ramp will fall apart and crash to the ground, with you standing on it. If you fall more than three levels, you'll perish.

Another basic structure you'll definitely want to become a pro at building very quickly is four walls around yourself. This is done using four vertical wall tiles and the directional controls on your controller or keyboard.

Build a bridge the same way as you'd build a ramp but use the horizontal wall tile instead of a ramp/stair-shaped tile.

When you come across a chest, Loot Llama, or supply drop that's out in the open, or if an enemy is shooting at you, quickly surrounding yourself with walls will offer shielding, at least for a few extra seconds, so you can escape. However, with the right weapons, an enemy can typically destroy your structures, especially if they're made from wood (shown here).

A wooden wall can withstand just 200 HP worth of damage before being destroyed. A stone wall can withstand 300 HP worth of damage from an incoming attack, while a metal wall can withstand 400 HP of damage from an incoming attack.

When you collect traps, Cozy Campfires, Launch Pads, and certain other loot items, they do not take up slots within your backpack's inventory. Instead, these items become accessible from Building mode. To use these items, they must be stored in your backpack's inventory, and then selected from the Building menu. On the left, a Launch Pad has been selected from the Building menu (seen near the bottom-right corner of the screen). It is being positioned on top of a flat floor tile.

In the bottom-right corner of the screen (on a Nintendo Switch and PS4, for example), notice the Trap icon that's displayed to the right of the four building tile options is selected. As a result, the trap can be placed against a wall or floor, for example. This is shown within the screenshot above on the right.

How to Build a 1x1 Fortress

A 1x1 fortress is simply four walls around you, with a ramp in the center, that goes up multiple levels. Using wood allows you to build with the greatest speed, but using metal offers the greatest protection. Keep practicing until you're able to build this type of fortress very quickly, without having to think too much about it.

Here's how to build a 1x1 fortress:

Especially if you're building on an uneven surface, consider starting with a floor tile on the ground.

Next, build four vertical walls so they surround you.

In the center, build a ramp. As the ramp is being constructed, jump on it.

Keep repeating this process to add levels to your fort. You can build as high as you need to, but in most situations, three or four levels is adequate.

At the top, consider adding pyramid-shaped roof pieces all around the roof for added protection when you peek out. However, if you need protection from directly above as well, add a flat roof or a pyramid-shaped roof piece directly over your head.

Surrounding the top of the 1x1 fort with pyramid-shaped tiles gives you objects to hide behind if you're peeking out from the top in order to shoot at enemies below.

This is what a three level 1x1 fortress looks like from the outside. Keep in mind, because it's made of wood (and not stone or metal), it would offer limited protection from an incoming attack, especially if more powerful explosive weapons are used to attack and attempt to destroy it.

How to Use Edit Mode to Add Windows, Doors, and More

Once you've built a structure out of wood, metal, and/or stone, you're able to enter into Edit mode in order to modify certain tiles, such as walls, floors, or ceilings. This is useful if you want to add a door or window, or create an opening and then expand your structure.

To enter into Edit mode, face a building tile that's been constructed. Shown here is one of the bottom walls of a 1x1 fortress. Press the appropriate button to enter into Edit mode. On a Nintendo Switch, for example, it's the "A" button. The controller or keyboard key you need to press will be displayed above the Edit icon that appears.

Once in Edit mode, the building tile you're facing turns blue and is divided into segments. Using the directional controls, start by pointing to one segment (box) and use the Confirm command. If you're building a window, you're all set. However, to build a door, you'll need to highlight and select two squares of the building tile (one on top of the other).

To continue building a door, select the second square on the tile, either above or below the first one you selected.

With both tiles selected, select the Confirm option.

In a few seconds, the door will be built. You're now able to open and close it, just as you would any other door in the game. Keep in mind, anyone else who approaches can also open the door to enter your structure.

Learning how to build, and then practicing until you're able to build extremely quickly is essential. Equally important, however, is to practice using Edit mode, so you're able to modify your structures quickly and efficiently during matches.

This is what a window looks like when it's built into a vertical wall. Use a window to peek out, or to point your weapon and snipe at enemies.

Anytime you build a window into a structure, just as you can see and shoot out, your enemies can see in and shoot through the window to attack you.

While in Building mode, you can clear four out of nine squares in order to create an arched opening.

This type of arched opening provides an easy way to expand your structure outwards with additional building. Of course, until you've done the additional building, the large opening within the structure leaves you potentially vulnerable to an incoming attack, with no protection except for your soldier's own health and shields.

Anytime you build a structure with a floor/ceiling tile (as opposed to a pyramid-shaped tile) as the floor or ceiling, enter into Edit mode to add a hole, so you can easily travel upwards or downwards within your fortress.

Here's a two-level fortress that was built next to a preexisting structure, and then linked to that structure with a bridge. This is an example of a structure that was built outward (to become wider) as opposed to taller. Adopting this type of building strategy is useful because someone attacking your structure can't determine from the outside where you're hiding on the inside, unless you peek out. This enables you to move around and stay safer longer during an incoming attack. Of course, building the fortress from stone or metal would provide much more protection than a structure built from wood.

After creating a multilevel structure or fortress, use Edit mode to create a hole in the floor or ceiling (when a flat floor/ceiling tile was used), so you can quickly drop downward or climb upward. When in Edit mode, build a one-box window in the floor or ceiling tile.

Use Your Creativity to Build More Elaborate Structures

Taking full advantage of the four different shaped building tiles and Edit mode, use your own creativity to come up with structure designs that:

- Provide protection from incoming attacks.
- Offer a good view of your surroundings from the top.

- Allow you to be higher up than your opponents, so you can shoot at them from above.
- Provide a place to safely hide, so you can use loot items to replenish your health and shields prior to launching an attack.
- Use a weapon with a scope to accurately shoot at enemies from a distance, while being protected.

In addition to doing your own experimentation, one excellent strategy for obtaining the best structure design ideas is to watch other players. For example, once you get defeated during a match, instead of immediately returning to the Lobby, stick around and take advantage of Spectator mode, so you can watch the rest of the match and see how other players handle themselves.

Another option is to watch YouTube videos produced by expert *Fortnite: Battle Royale* players, or to watch live streams of highly ranked players participating in matches on Twitch.tv. When you do this, pay extra attention to their building technique as they enter into the End Game portion of a match.

Building Advice When Preparing for the End Game

It's a common End Game strategy for players who make it into the Final Circle to build a large and sturdy fortress from which they can launch attacks on the remaining enemy soldiers using projectile explosive weapons, such as a grenade launcher or rocket launcher.

In order to build an elaborate fortress, and be able to repair it as needed during the match, you'll need to collect an abundance of resources. Plan ahead and collect or harvest up to 1,000 wood, stone, and metal prior to entering into the End Game. The longer you wait to collect the needed resources, the more dangerous it becomes, because you'll be in closer proximity to skilled enemies who will attack you while you're harvesting resources.

Along with having adequate levels of resources, make sure that within your backpack's inventory, you have the loot items and weapons you'll need to launch attacks (using a weapon with a scope or a projectile explosive weapon), and to replenish your health and shields as needed, so you can survive longer.

About halfway through each match, start thinking about the End Game and preparing for it. By defeating enemies in the later stages of a match, but prior to the End Game, you're able to grab all of the weapons, ammo, loot items, and resources that they've collected. This is a great way to build your arsenal and ensure you go into the End Game nicely equipped with resources.

If you haven't collected the powerful weapons you'll need during the End Game, and you don't necessarily want to risk engaging in battles before you absolutely have to, consider finding and using Vending Machines to stock up on weapons and needed loot items. Making purchases from Vending Machines requires using some of your resources, so plan accordingly.

How and Where to Build Your Final Fortress

As you enter into the Final Circle, and the End Game portion of a match begins, you'll be in relatively close proximity to the most skilled and cunning gamers remaining in the match. The Final Circle will be relatively small, so it's essential that you choose the best possible location to build your fortress.

Do not build in the center of the Final Circle. While this will give you 360-degree access to enemies around you, it'll also make you the center of attention, and the first enemy that the remaining soldiers will simultaneously attack. You're much better off choosing a location that's not centralized, so you can hang back a bit while the remaining soldiers fight among themselves and use up their ammunition and remaining resources. Then you can launch your attacks on whoever is left.

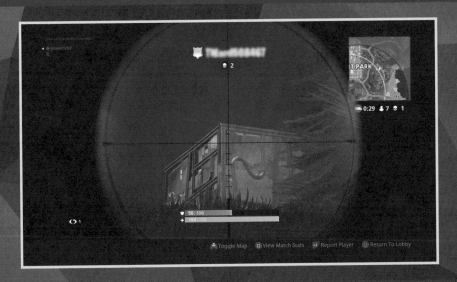

If you have a weapon with a scope in your arsenal, use it to zoom in and spy on your enemies from a distance, and then plan your strategy for attack. Seeing that this fort is made of metal, using the ammo from a sniper rifle probably won't penetrate the walls fast enough to hit your opponent. Instead, once you see what you're facing, consider using a projectile explosive weapon to take out the enemy fortress and whoever is inside, without having to leave the safety of your own fortress.

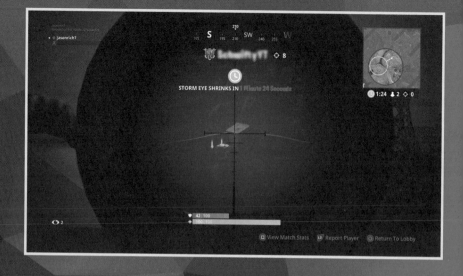

Using a weapon with an infrared scope attached allows you to see an enemy's heat signature, even if you can't actually see the enemy hiding behind an object, for example.

You'll often need to build with your back to the storm. Don't forget, soldiers can remain alive in the storm for short periods of time, so it's possible for someone to enter into the storm on purpose in order to reposition themselves in a way that they can emerge from the storm and sneak up behind you to launch a surprise attack. (You can do the same to your opponents.)

As you're choosing a design for your final fortress, make sure you can see immediately below you. It's common for enemies to leave the safety of their own fortresses and to rush enemy fortresses in order to launch close-range attacks with their most powerful weapons. Knowing this is a possibility, your arsenal should include at least one powerful weapon that's effective at close- to mid-range.

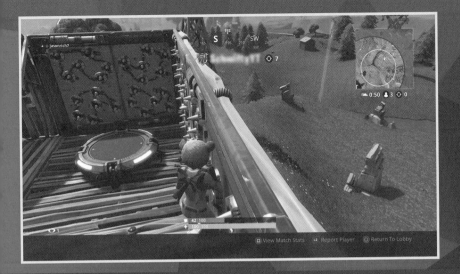

Consider placing a launch pad within your fortress. When you step on the launch pad, your soldier will fly upward. This allows you to get a bird's-eye view of your surroundings and determine where the final few enemy soldiers may be hiding. While in the air, travel straight up, look around, and then drop back down into your fortress.

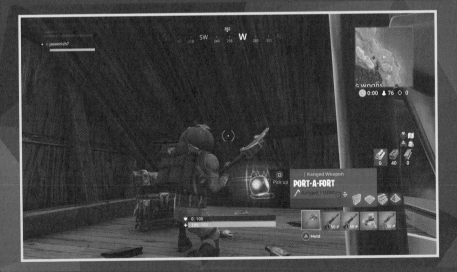

If you get yourself into a pinch during the End Game, and your fortress gets destroyed (but you manage to escape), or you forgot to collect enough resources to build a proper fortress, this is when using a Port-A-Fort can come in extremely handy. This is a rare loot item you can collect.

Once you have a Port-A-Fort stored in your backpack, activate it when it's needed at any time during a match. When you do, a metal fortress is instantly built around you, and thanks to the tires that come inside the fort, you can bounce to the top of it easily.

End Game Strategies for Defending, Repairing, or Abandoning Your Fortress

Each tile your structures or fortresses are built with has a specific HP that translates directly to the level of damage it can withstand before getting demolished. Keeping this in mind, it's important to understand that if the fortress you build during the End Game is not built with metal, it likely will not be able to withstand a direct hit from a projectile explosive weapon. While inside a fortress or structure, if it gets attacked, you'll typically have a few seconds to decide if you want to rebuild and repair the damage as it occurs or evacuate the structure altogether.

If you stick around and try to quickly rebuild, while in Building mode you can't use any weapons, so four factors need to be considered.

- Do you have enough resources to rebuild and repair the damage?

- Can you very quickly switch between Building mode and Combat mode, so you can counterattack enemies, especially if someone is rushing your fortress?
- Do you have the right weapons (and ammo) on hand to defend yourself?
- Will you be able to maintain a height advantage if you keep building, repairing, and defending your fortress?

Depending on how savvy your final opponents are, you may find yourself in an extremely small Final Circle. In this situation, it will become a vertical battle, as one enemy will literally be on top of the other(s). Having the height advantage will help here but having a powerful short-range weapon that you're really good at aiming with will often allow you to win the match. As you can see from the location map, the Final Circle is miniscule and surrounds the one remaining fortress. This final battle between these two soldiers came down to a close-range firefight that required perfect aim and split-second timing.

If your fortress gets destroyed, or you choose to forego building one during the End Game, you can still win the match. In this situation, you'll need to rush enemy fortresses, one at a time, and engage in close-range battles. Having grenades, clingers, and other explosives will help, as will powerful weapons that are good at close- to mid-range. The trick is to tiptoe as you approach an enemy fortress, so hopefully you won't be seen or heard.

With just four soldiers remaining in the match, the Final Circle is still pretty large. This soldier is using a projectile explosive weapon to blast away the small wooden fortresses where at least one remaining soldier is hiding. A wooden 1x1 fortress is no match for a rocket launcher.

Here, just two soldiers remain in the match, and both had their fortresses or hiding places destroyed. Thus, the winner was determined as a result of a very quick, close-range fight. The gamer with the quickest reflexes and best aim ultimately won.

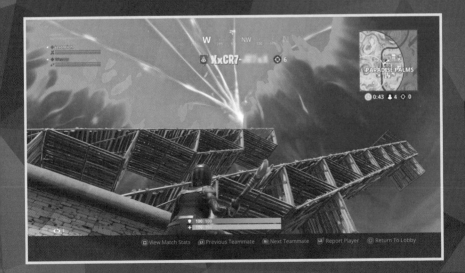

Instead of basic ramps, use your creativity and some extra resources to build reinforced ramps that can withstand attacks from stronger weapons.

SECTION 5

DISCOVER THE ARSENAL OF WEAPONS AND LOOT ITEMS AVAILABLE ON THE ISLAND

At any given time, the island contains hundreds of different types of weapons to collect, store in your backpack, and then use against adversaries.

The weapon categories these firearms and explosives typically fall into include: Assault Rifles, Grenade Launchers, Grenades, Miniguns, Pistols, Rocket Launchers, Shotguns, SMGs (Sub Machine Guns), and Sniper Rifles.

Many *Fortnite* gamers agree that the most useful weapon to master using is any type of shotgun. There are many types to choose from, and shotguns are more powerful than a pistol. When viewing the Backpack

Inventory screen, details about the selected weapon/item you're hold-ing are displayed. Here, details about the Pump Shotgun are displayed.

Shotguns can be used in close-range or mid-range combat situations, or even at a distance. (From a distance, they're harder to aim accurately than a rifle with a scope, for example.) When using a shotgun, always try for a headshot to inflict the most damage.

Each category of weapon can be used for a different purpose. Based on the type of enemy encounter you're experiencing at any given moment, it's essential that you choose the most appropriate weapon at your dis-posal. Before engaging in a firefight, consider:

- The types of weapons currently in your backpack and available to you.
- The amount of ammo you currently have for each weapon. (Be sure to pick up as much ammo as you can throughout each match.)
- The distance you are from your opponent.
- Your surroundings, and whether or not your weapon will need to destroy a barrier, fortress wall, or shielding before it can inflict damage on an enemy.
- Your own skill level as a gamer, and your speed when it comes to selecting, targeting/aiming, and then firing your weapon.

In each weapon category, up to a dozen or more different types of weapons may become accessible to you. Epic Games regularly tweaks the selection of weapons available, as well as the capabilities of each weapon.

Three Tips to Improve Your Shooting Accuracy

Regardless of which weapon you're using, your aim improves when you're crouching down and press the Aim button for the weapon you're using.

While it's often necessary to be running or jumping at the same time you're firing a weapon, your accuracy improves when you're standing still. It improves even more by pressing the Aim button before pressing the Trigger button.

You almost always have an advantage when you're higher up than your opponent and shooting in a downward direction.

Understand How Weapons Are Rated and Categorized

While every weapon has the ability to cause damage and defeat your adversaries, each is rated based on several criteria, including its rarity. Weapons are color-coded with a hue around them to showcase their rarity.

Weapons with a **grey** hue are "Common."

Weapons with a **green** hue are "Uncommon."

Weapons with a **blue** hue are "Rare."

Weapons with a **purple** hue are "Epic."

"Legendary" weapons (with an **orange** hue) are hard to find, extra powerful, and very rare. If you're able to obtain one, grab it!

It is possible to collect several of the same weapon, but each could have a different rarity. So, if you collect two of the same weapon, and one is rare, but the second is legendary, definitely keep the legendary weapon and trade the other for something else when you find a replacement.

The rarity of a weapon contributes heavily to its Damage Per Second (DPS) Rating. Thus, the DPS Rating for a legendary weapon is much higher than the DPS Rating for an identical weapon that has a common rarity, for example.

DPS Rating—This stands for "Damage Per Second." Use this rating to help estimate a weapon's power. It does not take into account things like accuracy of your aim, or the extra damage you can inflict by making a headshot, for example. In general, DPS is calculated by multiplying the damage the weapon can cause by its fire rate.

Damage Rating—A numeric rating, based on how much potential damage a weapon can cause per direct hit.

Fire Rate—This refers to the number of bullets fired per second. Some of the most powerful weapons have a slow Fire Rate, so to inflict the most damage, your aim needs to be perfect. Otherwise, during the time it takes in between shots, your enemy could move, or launch their own counterattack.

MAG (Magazine) Capacity—This is the total number of ammunition rounds (or bullets) the weapon can hold at once, before it needs to be reloaded. Reloading a weapon takes valuable time, during which your soldier will be vulnerable to attack. Your enemy could also move, meaning you'll need to re-aim your weapon.

Reload Time—The number of seconds it takes to reload the weapon, assuming you have replacement ammo available. Some of the most powerful weapons have a very slow reload time, so if your shooting accuracy isn't great, you'll be at a disadvantage.

There are plenty of websites, including: IGN.com (www.ign.com/wikis/fortnite/Weapons), Gameskinny.com (www.gameskinny.com/9mt22/complete-fortnite-battle-royale-weapons-stats-list), and RankedBoost.com (https://rankedboost.com/fortnite/best-weapons-tier-list), that provide the current stats for each weapon offered in *Fortnite: Battle Royale*, based on the latest tweaks made to the game. Just make sure when you look at this information online, it refers to the most recently released version of the game.

Choose Your Arsenal Wisely

Based on where you are, what challenges you're currently encountering, and what you anticipate your needs will be, stock your backpack with the weapons and tools you believe you'll need.

At any time, your soldier's backpack can hold six items (including the pickaxe). That leaves five slots in which you can carry different types of guns, alternative weapons (such as Traps, Remote Explosives, or Grenades), and/or loot (such as Med Kits, Chug Jugs, Shield Potions, Bandages, or Slurp Juice). Make smart inventory decisions throughout each match. The Backpack Inventory screen allows you to view what you have, plus organize the backpack's contents.

During a match, check your Backpack Inventory screen to learn more about each of the weapons you're carrying, and to determine how much of each type of ammunition you have on hand. From this screen, it's also possible to reorganize the backpack's contents, so it becomes faster and easier to grab the weapons or items you tend to use the most frequently.

Each time Epic Games releases an update, new weapons are introduced. As part of one update in late June, as Season 4 was winding down, the Dual Pistols were added to the game (as one weapon) and quickly became a popular weapon of choice for many players. Keep in mind, this weapon packs a wallop, but because you're using two guns at once, it uses twice the amount of ammo with each shot, compared to a regular pistol, for example.

Loot Items Are Extremely Useful

There are several ways to find and collect loot items, including:

- They're sometimes found out in the open, lying on the ground, behind objects, inside buildings or structures, as well as on top of or inside vehicles, for example.
- They're often found within chests, Supply Drops, and Loot Llamas.
- If an enemy is defeated and was carrying any loot items, they're dropped to the ground when the soldier is eliminated from the match.
- They can be purchased from Vending Machines.

A Supply Drop is seen here falling from the sky.

There are more than two dozen different types of loot items available in the game at any given time. Some of these items, like Apples, Bandages, Chug Jugs, Cozy Campfires, and Med Kits, are used to replenish a soldier's health by a predetermined amount. Each takes time to either consume or use, during which time a soldier is defenseless and vulnerable to attack. It's important to utilize these items only when it's safe, and your soldier is in a secluded area, or you're surrounded by walls. Here, a Cozy Campfire is being used to help replenish the soldier's health.

Chug Jugs, Mushrooms, and Shield Potions, for example, are used to activate or replenish a soldier's shields. (When a Chug Jug is consumed, both a soldier's HP and Shields are boosted to a maximum of 100). Slurp Juice adds up to 25 points to a soldier's Health meter and Shields meter.

Displayed at the bottom-center of the screen (on most gaming platforms), a soldier's Health meter is displayed as a green bar. When a soldier's shields are active, the Shields meter is displayed directly above the Health meter as a blue-colored bar. No matter what you use or consume, neither meter can go higher than 100. At the start of each match, a soldier's Health meter is at 100 and their Shields meter is at zero.

Loot items including Boogie Bombs, Bouncer Traps, Clingers, Grenades, Impulse Grenades, Remote Explosives, Stink Bombs, and Traps are all types of weapons that are not guns, but that can be used highly effectively and strategically in battle.

Port-A-Forts, Launch Pads, and Shopping Carts are among the other rare, but extremely useful, tools that sometimes become available during matches.

A Port-A-Fort creates an instant metal fort, while a Launch Pad catapults a soldier into the air to get a quick look around (and travel a good distance). Shopping Carts are used to move around the island quickly, as are ATKs. When you build a Port-A-Fort and jump to the top of it, immediately go into Build mode, and create one metal floor tile. Place it on the floor to keep enemy soldiers from entering the fort behind you to attack.

All Terrain Karts Offer a Great Way to Get Around

One of the most awesome additions to *Fortnite: Battle Royale* came at the start of Season 5 when All Terrain Karts (ATKs) were added to the game. Up to four squad members can ride in a single golf cart and travel around the island quickly.

The roof of the ATK works just like a Bounce Pad. Jump on it and your soldier will soar upwards into the sky. Another great thing about ATKs is that you can run over enemy soldiers and cause them damage. Just be careful, because they can shoot back. The soldier who is driving an ATK can't shoot a weapon at the same time. These vehicles can travel almost anywhere, and it's really fun when they go airborne. You'll need to practice driving in order to perform Power Slides and other slick maneuvers. Get some practice on the racetrack that's part of Paradise Palms (at map coordinates J6.5).

In addition to Shopping Carts and ATKs, another way to get around the island faster is to step directly into a rift. These are great for exploring, or to make an emergency escape if you're being beaten during a firefight.

SECTION 6

FORTNITE: BATTLE ROYALE RESOURCES

Pro gamers around the world have created YouTube channels, online forums, and blogs focused exclusively on *Fortnite: Battle Royale*. Plus, you can watch pro players compete online and describe their best strategies or check out the coverage of *Fortnite: Battle Royale* published by leading gaming websites and magazines.

On YouTube (www.youtube.com) or Twitch.TV (www.twitch.tv/directory/game/Fortnite), in the Search field, enter the search phrase "*Fortnite: Battle Royale*" to discover many game-related channels, live streams, and prerecorded videos.

Be sure to check out these awesome online resources that will help you become a better *Fortnite: Battle Royale* player:

WEBSITE OR YOUTUBE CHANNEL NAME	DESCRIPTION	URL
Fandom's *Fortnite* Wiki	Discover the latest news and strategies related to *Fortnite: Battle Royale*.	http://fortnite.wikia.com/wiki/Fortnite_Wiki
FantasticalGamer	A popular YouTuber who publishes *Fortnite* tutorial videos.	www.youtube.com/user/FantasticalGamer
FBR Insider	The *Fortnite: Battle Royale Insider* website offers game-related news, tips, and strategy videos.	www.fortniteinsider.com

(Continued on next page)

Fortnite Scout	Check your personal player stats, and analyze your performance using a bunch of colorful graphs and charts. Also check out the stats of other *Fortnite: Battle Royale* players.	www.fortnitescout.com
Fortnite Stats & Leaderboard	This is an independent website that allows you to view your own *Fortnite*-related stats or discover the stats from the best players in the world.	https://fortnitestats.com
Game Informer Magazine's *Fortnite* Coverage	Discover articles, reviews, and news about *Fortnite: Battle Royale* published by *Game Informer* magazine.	www.gameinformer.com/search/searchresults.aspx?q=Fortnite
Game Skinny Online Guides	A collection of topic-specific strategy guides related to *Fortnite*.	www.gameskinny.com/tag/fortnite-guides/
GameSpot's *Fortnite* Coverage	Check out the news, reviews, and game coverage related to *Fortnite: Battle Royale* that's been published by GameSpot.	www.gamespot.com/fortnite
IGN Entertainment's *Fortnite* Coverage	Check out all IGN's past and current coverage of *Fortnite*.	www.ign.com/wikis/fortnite
Jason R. Rich's Website and Social Media Feeds	Share your *Fortnite: Battle Royale* game play strategies with this book's author and learn about his other books.	www.JasonRich.com www.FortniteGameBooks.com Twitter: @JasonRich7 Instagram: @JasonRich7
Microsoft's Xbox One *Fortnite* Website	Learn about and acquire *Fortnite: Battle Royale* if you're an Xbox One gamer.	www.microsoft.com/en-US/store/p/Fortnite-Battle-Royalee/BT5P2X999VH2
MonsterDface YouTube and Twitch.tv Channels	Watch video tutorials and live game streams from an expert *Fortnite* player.	www.youtube.com/user/MonsterdfaceLive www.Twitch.tv/MonsterDface

Ninja	Check out the live and recorded game streams from Ninja, one of the most highly skilled *Fortnite: Battle Royale* players in the world on Twitch.tv and YouTube.	www.twitch.tv/ ninja_fortnite_hyper www.youtube.com/user/ NinjasHyper
Nomxs	A YouTube and Twitch.tv channel hosted by online personality Simon Britton (Nomxs). He too is one of *Fortnite*'s top-ranked players.	https://www.youtube.com/ watch?v=np-8cmsUZmc or www.twitch.tv/ videos/259245155
Official Epic Games YouTube Channel for *Fortnite: Battle Royale*	The official *Fortnite: Battle Royale* YouTube channel.	www.youtube.com/user/ epicfortnite

Your Fortnite Adventure Continues . . .

Hold on to your controller, keyboard, or touchscreen, because there's so much more new and exciting *Fortnite: Battle Royale* gaming in store for you as time goes on! Epic Games continues to update this mega-popular game with sometimes dramatic alterations to the island map; by introducing challenging new game play modes; by revealing exciting new storylines and subplots; by adding powerful new weapons and innovative types of new loot; and by making available eye-catching ways to showcase your soldier's appearance (with outfits, back bling pickaxes, gliders, emotes, and other customizable elements).

To make sure that your *Fortnite: Battle Royale* never becomes boring, predictable, or easy to master, new game play modes and competitions are introduced on a regular basis, while the Solo, Duos, and Squads modes continue to be tweaked to add new levels of challenges and excitement to them.

Plus, anytime you gather one or more friends to compete with you in the Duos or Squads game play modes (accessible from the Lobby), for example, the challenges and unpredictability within the game increase dramatically. Teamwork (including constant communication with your allies) becomes vitally important.

Now that you've discovered tons of useful strategies to follow, what will make you a truly awesome gamer is a ton of practice! Remember, when it comes to building on the island, speed is essential!

So, as the Battle Bus departs with your soldier on it, good luck, and more importantly, have fun!

Jason R. Rich, the author of the guide you're currently reading, has teamed up with Sky Pony Press (an imprint of Skyhorse Publishing), to write an entire series of unofficial, full-color *Fortnite: Battle Royale* strategy guides (each sold separately).

To get your hands on these information-packed strategy guides, visit your favorite bookstore, or when visiting Amazon.com or BN.com, within the Search field, type, "*Fortnite, Jason R. Rich*" to find and order the latest guides. You can also visit www.FortniteGameBooks.com for more information.